THE MERCHANT OF FEATHERS

ACKNOWLEDGEMENTS

Grateful acknowledgement is made to the editors of the following publications in which versions of some of the poems in this collection first appeared:

Small Axe: A Caribbean Journal of Criticism; *Cave Canem Anthology XII: Poems 2008 and 2009* (Aquarius Press, 2012); *So Much Things to Say* (Akashic Books, 2010); *Jubilation* (Peepal Tree Press, 2012); *AfroBeat Journal*.

This book was only possible because of the unconditional love and support I continue to receive from my mom, Madge Shirley, my sister and brother-in-law, Tanice and Abner Gonsalves, and my niece who keeps me smiling, Marley Rose Gonsalves. Thanks to my circle of friends and relatives – the village that props me up. Thanks to AJ for showing up just when I needed him and for winning my heart. Blessings to Marva for always having my back. Thank you to Lorna Goodison, Mervyn Morris, and Michael Bucknor for their critical feedback and their words of encouragement. Thanks to Kei Miller for regaling me with the most hilarious anecdotes that often inspire me to write. My heart is full of gratitude for Jeremy, Hannah, Adam, and the entire Peepal Tree Press family. Thanks also to Cave Canem for the gift of community.

THE MERCHANT OF FEATHERS

TANYA SHIRLEY

PEEPAL TREE

First published in Great Britain in 2014
Peepal Tree Press Ltd
17 King's Avenue
Leeds LS6 1QS
UK

ISBN 13: 9781845232337

Supported using public funding by
ARTS COUNCIL
ENGLAND

CONTENTS

III: Let This Be Your Praise

Where I come from,
old women bind living words
 across their flat chests,
inscribe them on their foreheads,
and in the palms of their hands.
If you don't have the eye
to you they just look like
third world women with nothing much.

Lorna Goodison, *Goldengrove: New and Selected Poems*

This time there was no beak,
no little bloody head, no bony
claw, no loose wing – only a small
pile of feathers without substance or center.

Gerald Stern, *This Time: New and Selected Poems*

In Memory of Luna May Dorothy Beckford
and Carlton Washington Beckford

THE ALPHABET OF SHAME

THE ALPHABET OF SHAME

You must have been proud:
first on the street to acquire a satellite dish.
How far you had come from country boy
working at the post office to save
for a red bicycle you pushed up hill, afraid
riding would break it.
Now laughing in a circle of new friends,
gin and tonic in hand, king of your landscaped yard,
you say, "I love looking in the *Arbit*,
seeing all the channels to choose from."
She says, "It's *Orbit* not *Arbit*."
She is ten and cheeky, always first in class,
well, except that one time she came second;
you crushed her report card into a brittle bomb,
threw it out the third-storey window, startling the dogs.
Your friends laugh and you laugh louder.
Ten minutes later she is skipping in the corridor
between the den and kitchen. You catch her.
"Never, ever embarrass me!" you say,
fingers like forceps squeezing her chubby cheek.
Years of ballet and still she is storing fat.
"Now go to your room and stay there!"
She watches the party from a small window,
face sandwiched between burglar bars,
forlorn but not foreseeing
that this is the beginning
of a life sentence.

HOW DREAMS GROW FAT AND DIE

All summer I practised walking
in wooden-tip ballet shoes,
pretended God was pulling me up,
ten-year-old marionette,
steps stuttering from room to room.

Flat-footed I traced grout lines
in our kitchen with encyclopedias
on my head, balancing dreams of
twirling off stage into the sails
of standing ovations.

In September, you told my mother I
was too fat to be a ballerina.
You, of faux British accent and hollowed
collar bones I imagined were tea cups.

You, who wanted a *kukumkum* orchestra,
a herd of bones gliding under
the baton of your arms.

You, who illustrated to my mother
my incompetence by drawing a circle
in the air. I was the round nightmare
landing heavy in the melody of grand jetés.

You could keep me back with the younger
girls, maybe in a year or two I would shed
the fat, reverse blossom into fragrant bud,

or I could donate my tutu now
to the kingdom of dust cloths, hang my ballet
shoes by their wooden-tip necks.

In dreams I am a feather, buoyed and buoyant
and you are the barbed wire that kills me.

SUMMER DAYS

Our house sat on a hill,
three-storey remnant of whites
who made money here
but fled to Florida
in the '70s when independence
was fresh in our mouths
and riots still smelled
like burning cane.

As a girl in her prime,
I would stand on the upper balcony,
watch the neighbourhood boys play ball,
while wearing a brown towel on my head;
clasped in the back,
the cascading cotton –
my very own ponytail.

I would paint my lips
hibiscus pink, pull a maxi skirt up
into a sleeveless dress,
twirl and preen and pose
on my balcony,
as years before me
some white girl did.

RECOMPENSE

Remember how Janet get up in history class and say she not black and we laugh and tell her fi sit her black backside down but Janet say we too fool for school; she half Scottish. And somebody tug on Janet plait and say look how yuh head tough and Janet say don't make that fool you; naked eye don't see the blood. In 18-something her great great great somebody step off a boat and dig up her great great great somebody out the cane field to test the sweetness of local sugar (no sense buying puss in a bag) and she not letting Scotland get away scot-free; she laying claim to that money that build bronze statues & columned empires on cobblestone streets and she say bet you when Scotland issue apology and say all half-breeds line up here for recompense, all a we who black and a bray like ass going start sing different tune but she going be first in line. All along she singing the same thing: there is money in this blood, money in this blood. And somebody in Janet family must've been drawing a family tree because she swear is Scotland her father people come from. And we laugh and ask Janet if she sure is not Ireland or England. We say, Janet sit down, yuh can't even find we own Clarendon on Miss Dawson' map. When we graduate, news fly on a paper plane tell we that Janet went to London to study but money run out and she couldn't find not one white family and, Lord have mercy, we hear she turn all shade of black.

FLOWER GIRL

Her mother placed two red cushions
on a dining room chair, lifted her high
into the air, then settled her atop with
a firm hand and a kiss on the forehead.

The hot comb began its virgin trek
through tangled coils; the brown child
knitted her brows and before the comb
could straighten a new tuft of tight curls

she released a howl, the kind that scares
the prey and shatters ribs on its way
out the body – the body skilled in contortion –
pushing the limit of limbs and restraints.

You can't be a flower girl with nappy hair.
You want to spoil your aunty's wedding?
Is shame you want to shame we?

How much more shame could this child cause?
Wasn't it enough that now they knew
she was part animal, capable of breaking
atoms and dreams with her screams?

The hairdresser cooed and cajoled,
but she was no match for this child
who had not yet learned that vanity
will make women walk through fire.

The child threw herself to the ground,
yanked off her yellow dress, heaved
and heaved, rolled and spun her eyes
into half moons, the room growing red.

Give the pickney two good lick!
Is them kind of pickney turn round box
them own mother and father.

But the poor mother was transfixed.
Each convulsion a rip in the umbilical cord.
Where did a child like this come from and how
do you mother this?

The child spewed vomit
on to the rug then gasped for air.
The army of aunts swooped down, carried her
into the tub, turned on the cold water full-force.

We rebuke you Satan! Jesus! Jesus!
We cast you out Satan! Jesus! Jesus!
Devil come out! Jesus! Jesus!

The child gripped the side of the tub, looked up
to the heavens hidden behind the ceiling,
then fell asleep, the aunts wondering,
What do we do with her hair?

SWEET SWEET JAMAICA

We cannot find our little girls
we cannot find our little boys

       We search all day
       we search all night

for their dangling plaits and rainbow beads
for their bobby socks and superman briefs

What are little girls made of?
Sugar and spice and army knives
bullets and broken glass

What are little boys made of?
Mongrel dog tails, slimy snails,
belt buckles and barbed wire wounds

       Have you looked in the sewer?
       Have you searched in the swamp?

Where daddies and mistresses and mommies
and neighbours stuff decapitated corpses
of little brown girls and little black boys

who can't play anymore on swings or in trees
in lanes or in puddles, in back rooms or front rooms

No marbles or dandy shandy
jump rope or bull in the pen
no hide and seek or

       big bird big bird
       in and out the window
       big bird big bird in and out the window

Our little girls are stuffed in small spaces
coming up on shore in plastic bags
burning in safe houses
hanging from burglar bars

Our little girls are lying in blood, their legs pried open

Our little boys lie in blood, butchered like cattle
Our little boys hang from street corners
Our little boys are on fire at our feet

When we find them, it is always too late
We hurl stones into the wind
We blow steam up media asses
We stand outside government houses

        and then we grow quiet
        like dust on the tombstones
        of little bones

"THE PEOPLE ARE DEADING"

Said by a woman interviewed by a reporter about her response to the Tivoli Gardens incursion when Jamaican police men and soldiers entered that community in search of Dudus Coke who was wanted for extradition to the USA. Her response was later put to music and became a YouTube sensation.

and we are laughing
at this sound bite played over sweet bass
spliced and digitized for YouTube consumption

but when the people were *deading*
we were hiding under king-sized beds
panic buttons strapped to our chests

just in case someone got the wrong address:
the police or the bad men, or the bad men
or the police. In that bullet-ridden dark

even teeth looked like dried blood
and you couldn't see anybody's soul
in the slant of seedy eyes.

No one was dying or crossing over,
passing or walking into the light;
no one had the benefit of a benediction.

The people were *deading*
like language ripped from a tongue
leaving clots of dry vowels in underground tunnels.

The people were *deading*
in a plague of fire bombs and a deluge of bullets;
in uniformed arbitrary tactics

20

boys, who were chased from birth
by the shadow of death, held hostage
by blind dollar bills and potbellied politicians,

were being blown out of their bodies
and only a woman like this one trapped
in a computer screen and a catchy rhythm

dares to look out at us and shatter
our silence and indifference, our stupid laughter
with her humble burial rites.

THE DAY I FELT LIKE MIGRATING
For D

Your father, still in church attire –
crisp pair of pants, long sleeve shirt
the grandchildren gave him this Christmas.

Your father, fresh from singing, baritone
still trembling in the rafters, still warm
from prayer and exiting-church-hugs.

Your father, elder appointed on this day
to deposit the tithes, too hefty for the
slender security of a church.

Your father, who walks with God
in his stride to the bank, is accosted
by a man witnesses later say looked

like he was asking for directions, but
he pulls a gun. Your father steps back
in defiance, pivoting on the certainty

of right over wrong.
He maintains his grip on the bag of fat
dollar bills. Your father is shot and still

he runs, holding on to what he knows
belongs to God, not this man
with the gospel of bullets.

Your father drives himself to the hospital.
In traffic, we never know how the man behind us
bleeds.

THE SEA

I am thinking about the sea. I am remembering a friend who fell into the water and the propeller tore open her arm. We sat helpless on the boat while the sea turned red. We were only twelve. She insisted I follow her into the emergency room. When the doctor removed the towel and I saw the muscles in her arm, like pink worms piled on a butcher's block, I fainted. The taste of the sugar and water is still fresh in my mouth. The guilt I felt for fainting, for not being the one who fell off, for not saving her mid-fall, is still raw. Some nights it sits beside me on the bed. I remember my parents' faces as they handed her over to her parents when we got back into town. For our entire eighth grade I could not look at her long arms. I could not look at her face. Years later when I looked at the scar on her arm, a curdled mass of flesh from under armpit to elbow, I thought, *This is what ruin looks like*. My father took my sister and me out on the boat the following weekend. He said we needed to conquer our fear. My mother stood at the water's edge and cried. My father made us steer the boat. He made us go fast. He took our hands and pushed them against the tide; the water was blood beneath my fingernails. My mother did not speak to him for weeks. He could not give us back what the sea had taken. My friend grew shorter with each passing year. She crawled into that scar. She did not take me with her. I am thinking about the sea, how deceptive blue is, how thirsty I have been.

WAITING FOR RAIN (AGAIN)

I am thinking of the drought, the parched earth
outside my door, the plant the gardener killed
with water from the pool; in desperate times,
we try everything. I have mastered the art of bathing
from a bucket. I know a lady with seven water tanks
in her forever-green backyard; she says they're not enough.
There are poor people in this country
who've never had running water, who carry pails
full from the river on their heads.
Sandwiched in pews, their only prayer is for rain
to start their produce growing again, perhaps
before the next set of school fees are due.
Poor people in thick circles dancing for rain.
Obeah men getting extra business for rain.
Still, it has not rained.
And who knew an empty tap could have me in tears.
Perhaps, I am grieving for all the dying things,
people in this desert looking out, looking in.
Perhaps, I am giving up myself as a tank, as a city river,
an oasis for all this thirst.
Let them come and drink of me, my brokenness
spilling in shards of tears.

SPELL #1

to be that desperate in love   *give him wine*

so uncertain of your hip's rhythm,
the sweet salt of your sweat

                                                give him sparkling wine

so certain this is the man
who walks on water in your dreams

                                                        in a blue goblet

you want him sewn into your skin

                                                        wine sweetened

his name like buttons on your ribs,
his mouth sprouting from your neck

                                        wine sweetened with your fresh

this is love, not madness
ask the moon if she could live without the sky

                                                wine sweetened with
                                        your fresh fingernail   trimmings

kiss the nail clipper: holiest of love spoons,
giver of reckless light

                                        finger nail trimmings drowning
                                                in the golden sea

EN ROUTE TO NEGRIL

For Nigel & Caroline

We both saw it:
a corpulent white bird in the middle of the street.
Had I been driving, I would have swerved
but you, in your masculine surety, knew
it would fly off before the impact of tires on flesh.
It did not.
Two thumps: right front tire, right back tire
and the rear vista was a canvas of feathers
free falling in the orange afternoon.
Your face creased in shock.
Maybe it was crippled? Why didn't it fly?
It must have seen this steel machine.
And some wicked streak in me rose up
and shouted: Bird Killer!
You had to pull over on the soft shoulder.
Death fogged the car but, not knowing,
the cane vendor sauntered over,
pressed his wares against the window.
I bought two bags.
Pushed a small piece into your mouth.
When we were children and our parents
took us for country trips, my father would drive
over mongooses just for sport.
As we drive off, I try not to look at you
with that view from the past.
It helps that on our return when I point out
the dried blood on the street and a solitary
white feather, you bow your head
as if in prayer.

MATIE SHALL NOT CONQUER

You know all men are weak.
You see the way she watches him, you imagine
she has a basket of red apples and a snake
coiled around her belly,
but this is the man who made you come
more times than you could count.
You are willing to use the wisdom of women
long dead to keep his eyes in your skin.

Light three blue candles:
the flickering will taper
the conflagration in your blood;
fight big fire with small fire.
Write his name and your name on a piece of paper.
Write her name on another; if you do not know it,
be patient, he will whisper it in his sleep.
On the third piece of paper, write three positive wishes
for your rival, all the time wishing the bitch well.
Negative thoughts are returned to sender.

Place one drop of clove oil on each piece.
Fold papers and put in an envelope – it should be white
like the dress you're wearing.
Keep it under your mattress for seven nights.
On the eighth night, when only the owl's eyes are upon you,
burn the envelope in a big, glass bowl.
Do not set your house on fire.
Scatter the ashes outside, far away from your dogs;
like ganja seeds, it will drive them crazy.

In the morning, he will come to you
with a rose in his mouth
and her name will be mud on the soles of his feet.

WHAT WORDS CAN DO

I.

"He died in a plane crash," she said.
No batting eyelids, no disingenuous smile,
no "just kidding" minutes later.
It was the other hairdressers who told me
she was lying:
"Is bruk up dem bruk up!"
I envied her the courage to kill off a man
just like that.
I have a long list of men I would like to murder,
to bury their ashes in the city's sewer
but I'm afraid I would hear them saying "sorry"
from the other side
and I'd want to put them back together again.

II.

My father has died; sucked into the underworld
of forgotten fish, he swims without any of us
breathing down his back.

III.

It is easier than I thought.
Although even death does not seem
like justice enough.

MAKING FAMILY

For Tanice, Abner and Marley Rose

On a Sunday drive through the valley
where your dream house lives,
a glimpse behind reveals a lonely deer
in the middle of the road.

I imagine he is tired of all the shrubbery,
brambles and moist beneath his feet.
Even a deer gets tired of habitual green, yearns
for the danger of brick walls, clumsy cars.

Our parents used to take us for Sunday drives.
Licking sloping ice cream cones we'd *ooh* and *aah*
at quaint villas and three-storeys perched precariously.
We were a family of four – mouth-stained and giddy.

Now, on my summer visit to Virginia where you live,
we are four once again: me, you, your husband and child.
We grow out of our parents' cocoons, we leave islands
and their dreams for us in our wake.

We traverse new paths, where in the rear-view a deer
stands as witness and I hold a malleable two-year-old's hand,
hoping one day she too will branch out and we who are left
at home, will grasp her yearning for a different view.

STANDING OUTSIDE THE CIRCLE

MONTEGO BAY

I'm dancing barefoot, toes
digging into the sand, for you.
You're locked in small talk
with a Rasta lady but your eyes
are facing my direction, perhaps
looking out to sea, trailing the water's
silver quilt for a song or signs of rain.
I imagine it is me you find
washed up like a pirate's treasure,
rolling my hips, rubbing the sweat
on my neck, the top of my breasts in slow
small circles, marking time with Marley,
when a friend says, "You don't wine to Bob."
But Bob would understand
what a woman has to do to hold a man
in this one room of sea and sky.

Each semaphore is for your unravelling.
This sped-up gyration for the thirst
in your eyes; this slowed down dip
and push back, roll and press forward
for the quiver in your lips,
their plumpness, their secrets, their grasp
on my nipple; this sideways rock and slither
for the girth of your hands; this slow skank backward
and forward for the smooth of your skin.

But it is not enough.
You'll remember your obligations: a wife
to return to, school fees to be paid, the high light
bill, a roof in need of repair, an ailing father,
the overgrown lawn, church on Sunday.
You'll turn your back and I'll continue to dance.

POETRY AT AN OVERSEAS PRISON

There was too much freedom in that prison,
only one guard to over two hundred men –
shirtless men with shuffling eyes
and knives for peeling oranges,
shears to shave and no bars, only sheets
swaying in makeshift cells.
Before we entered, we were told to act cool,
unafraid, reminded of our common humanity.
But we were five women in a sea of hungry men.
I could see them holding my flesh, tender
between their teeth.
I said, "I bring greetings from the land of Bob Marley."
They clapped and hooted, puffed on imaginary spliffs.
I sang "One Love" under my breath,
each word a rosary bead on the tongue.
I swear I only escaped uneaten
because my country preceded me and a man
kept his toe and suffered
sweet music that would, one day, save me.

AWAY FROM HOME

You hadn't heard from me in so long,
thought I had died or returned home.
The Islands is such a good place to live.

They were all the same to you.
I watch your lips move. The smell
of burned popcorn comes through the walls.
Your dirty talk drowns me.

Next door, they turn on the TV.
They will not hear the silence of my toes
curling, travelling to verandahs sprouting
sing-song accents and laughter,
easy banter blowing in the wind.
They will not hear my mind wander
to days spent under mango trees
or sipping beer at the beach.

They may hear me coming,
but they will not know how
it is tinged with sadness.
They may hear me peeing, purging
you out so quickly and surely,
from my slit, cut-eye.

STANDING OUTSIDE THE CIRCLE

Granny is propped up by cushions,
pillows; her grown children, grand children
shift her wig, tuck and untuck her frayed
floral blouse, rearrange the fall of her arms.

They place an open Bible in her lap.
One of them starts, "Remember the time…"
bending closer to Granny, beckoning her
to follow the dubious path of memory.

I have nothing to say to this configuration
of turgid flesh and mock uprightness.
I loved her from a distant place: the whitish
woman we'd visit every couple of years,

who spoke much louder than I expected,
whose fowl coop smelled so bad I'd retch
but hold it in my mouth until no one was looking.
My parents liked to think we had a bit of country in us.

My father would rub her feet and she'd show us
her photo albums, the crevices of her house
as if it were our first visit.
I stand in front of her now, her eyes puffed up

like poisoned fish; beneath her skin a blue-black
dye swims to the surface and just when my mother
says, "Say something nice to your granny,"
the undertakers enter the room with a long stretcher.

The women widen their circle, in unison they begin
the death howl; one falls to the floor – the self-appointed,
professional mourner. She rolls from side to side,
she curls in on herself, she spreads herself out:

a glorious spectacle in the fading afternoon.
Someone half shouts, half sings, "Granny dead,
Granny dead, Ohhh!" and the chorus – a cacophony
of flailing arms, nodding heads, wobbling legs – joins in.

I do not recognize my mother.

MESSAGE IN A DREAM

As I walk through a bazaar on the beach
where vendors sell fruits, fried fish, fragrant oils,
calabashes, hemp dresses, natural juices,
a woman walks out of the waves:
"I must read your palms, O woman of magic."
She pulls me down into the sand,
sits behind me, my back against her chest.
She puts my palms like cups into the cups
of her palms. We sway like sea-grape branches.
Vendors gather like apostles around us.
Lightning rises out of my palms
hits the water and the waves spit fire.
"You are too passionate," she whispers.
"You will kill things along the way."
I wake to the sound of the city's sirens
and my curtains dancing like wind parting
in the wake of a woman's leaving.

WHAT WE DO NOT SEE

There are days her spirit lays low –
a heaviness in her legs, the sheets like an anchor.
Those days her mind is a sieve that holds
only the memory of loss.
She wants to banish all men and their weapons
but she remains silent,
hates herself for the limpness of her tongue,
the way she curls caterpillar-like into herself.
Days like today she cannot fight the urge to keep
the dirty laundry hidden in brown, tidy baskets,
so she does nothing, simply allows the body
to lead and it plays dead out of self-defence.
Tomorrow, she will dress and face the customers,
the traffic, the family, careful to put on extra
make-up: bronze on her cheeks, green on her eyes,
red on her lips. She will laugh, opening her mouth
wide, swinging her head all the way back.
She will walk with a bounce and a swing and the world
will claim her as one of the living, not knowing
how close she lives to the ground,
dust always gathering in her mouth.

AGAIN

August

Beneath yards of white cotton
a fruit ripens in the heat.

You roll it on your tongue, tug
at it, find it fit to eat.

You wipe the sweat from your brow;
my mouth receives it as rain.

Each mouthful melts the small stone
he left to grow in my throat.

Country

On a bed of grass, you nuzzle between my thighs –
even the sun blushes.

Your hands – broad leaves that cocoon
my breasts against wind and rain.

You hear the river beneath my navel
running to your open mouth.

Open your eyes and feast; let this body
be an altar for new tears.

Morning

Beneath your sweet tongue lies
a black mamba, his poison the only thing true.

I watch you lick the spoon clean,
drifting from me and this place.

The salt smell clings to sheets, curtains, fingers.
My nose remembers.

Your mouth holds our fresh regret,
spits out new words formed in the dark.

WHEN THE WORLD IS SLEEPING

After lovemaking, in the pull and tug
of snoring and silence, they spoon
under the moon's blue blanket.
His dick is a dead man on her back.
She imagines the world he left behind:
small triumphs, gargantuan failures.
He is finally at peace, like a patient
unplugged from tubes and the world's pity.
Still on fire, her body cremates him.
What will she do with the ashes?
How does she convince his family
he died on his own volition?

But some nights
his dick on her back is a dead man
who didn't want to die.
His hate climbs into the calm after climax.
He wanted to return unwounded,
walk in the welcome home parade,
be knighted by the queen for his gallantry.

In the dark, she constructs a eulogy.
She tells all the men lined in pews down
her thighs, the holy women tucked behind
her knees, that loving is always the act
of dying and only the determined few breathe
themselves back to life.
It's not her fault he couldn't pull himself up.

SAID BY A DJ AT AN UPTOWN DANCE

Bruk off yuh head, mi buy it back a mawnin

And what is a woman's head, but dispensable?
A dutty wining machine, a hypnotist's string,
a windmill.

I want a man so rich
that when my head comes and goes
as it often does
and doesn't come back again
or when he grinds me into salt
or when his single eye sucks me in,
he can go to the store where women's heads are sold
and get me a new one.
A man so accommodating that he will love me
even in my new-headed body.
I imagine all new heads go through periods of adjustment.
During that time, he will settle for deep discussions
with my breasts and marvel at the acquiescing nature
of my tender parts.
Matter of fact, which woman really needs a head
unless she is proficient in giving head,
and keeping her mouth shut when she's not?

Mr. DJ, two headless women were found in Spanish Town;
kindly give their families some money and directions to the store.

THE MERCHANT OF FEATHERS II

is the mother whose son is found
in a *compromising position* with a man
in a university bathroom
and is beaten by security guards
who police anuses
while girls walk unguarded in the night
and a mob of educated fools chant
for more blood, more fire;
this is the mother who must put her son back together,
paint his wounds with gentian violet,
ice swollen tendons, protuberant eyes,
find the scars deeper than skin,
and like a seamstress mend what's broken within,
and when his father, who isn't worth two dry stones
or a shilling, sees his son on the news and appears
at her door to beat her son some more,
she will turn herself into serrated edges,
stand sharp and poised to kill,
for her son is her only gold,
and if the father's thirst for blood is too great
she will pacify him with what he needs
to prove he is not like his son;
in her, he will bury the fear.
And in the morning she will stir soft words
into the cornmeal porridge, carry it to her son's bed,
blow a benediction into each spoonful she brings
to his bruised and beautiful lips.

BEYOND THE AIDS HOSPICE

Even as it rains
your body burns
to a cinder;

the spirit, shocked
by fire, leaps from
your chest.

It flies past the laden
clouds, takes up
its new post:

tour guide to heaven,
showing men suddenly fat
again their new home.

ON A NEW KINGSTON CORNER

It was not her scanty attire that shocked me
(I imagine prostitutes face stiff competition),
it was the two black scandal bags,
one beside each foot, like weights pulling her
into the ground. Were those her bag of tricks?
I pictured purple boas, whips, vibrators, flavoured condoms.
But her scowl and the scar spread from right ear to chin,
her beaten-down loafers, plain black thong, no lace,
no frills, no neon lights like the crotchless ones
I saw once that said "Open 24 hours",
suggested with her you got basic service: a little head,
some missionary, definitely no taking it up the ass.
So what was in her bags?
A lifetime of being shuffled between baby fathers,
grandmothers, friends who switched to day jobs,
all of whom at one point or another put her out?
Eventually, even the benevolent expect payment
and a well frequented front was of no value.
I wonder what she's collected over the years,
deemed important enough to gain a spot in the tight
scandal bag space: a rosary from one of the missionaries
who tried to show her Mary and failed, a picture
of her mother who no doubt migrated and left her
with a grandmother who taught her early on
that demons were real and she was a demon child,
bruised fruit, cheap perfume, a letter from her eldest
child, a plastic cup, a tattered rag, a knife for dangerous
nights, some weed, a half-dead cell phone,
a long dress in case she changes her mind?

EVERY HOE HAVE HIM STICK A BUSH

Our resident mad man (I imagine every neighbourhood has one)
would wake us every Saturday morning with a barrage
of *bomboclaats*, *rassclaats* and other *claats*.
He was regular like the sound of my neighbour's washing
machine, crying children, her Spanish-speaking husband.
But I should have known insanity precludes consistency.
He's started to curse at least two days in the week,
sometimes early morning, sometimes late at night.
I lie awake wondering how long he'll take,
what new phrase he'll invent. Of late he's been shouting
(he's never quiet), *A wha' do you? Eeh? Eeh?*
There's never an answer, never another voice.
I imagine he's questioning himself.
Perhaps even in madness we're frustrated
with our shortcomings, struggling towards sanity,
the way the sane amongst us struggle against insanity.
I wonder what our neighbourhood would sound like without him.
I've always been drawn to public outbursts,
when we forget to leave the dirty linens inside,
when we need the world to witness our existence.
One Saturday morning a man came to the mad man's house,
(it's not really a house – he's the caretaker of an unfinished scheme,
a shrine to the economic downturn) warning him
to leave his woman alone. He banged on the zinc gate.
Said he knew his woman was in there with him even now.
I wondered if he had the wrong address. I dressed quickly.
Stood in the road with others brave enough to flaunt their nosiness.
After much machete wielding, banging, shouting and swearing,
he jumped on his bicycle, riding away in a defeated dirt cloud.
Soon the mad man emerged with a woman by his side.
She looked clean and not at all ugly. She avoided our eyes but he
walked towards us all the while screaming, *Wha' di rass unuh looking on?*
We dispersed quickly, smelling the violence on his tongue.
I returned to my house and the echo of my breathing.

IN TIMES OF TROUBLE

When you're so broken you don't know how to pray,
you spend hours orchestrating the significance
of bloodied feathers that seem to pop up everywhere.
You stare at the sky for hours watching blue
explode into orange at the tip of dusk.
You tattoo a neon sign on your forehead,
"Broken, please enter." You let men in hoping
they'll build mansions in the rubble of your arms.
You visit obeah women, hypnotists, priests, psychiatrists;
they can't put you back together again.
Not even the music riding in on Kingston's waves
can save you from drowning. You were born
broken unto a broken mother and a broken father.
Your umbilical cord was buried under a barren tree.
You will need God to interpret the language of death,
angels and ancestors to thunder their chests. You need
the most violent upheaval: to catch a fire and burn to nothing.

TEACHING *JANE EYRE*

Those first few weeks of dating
you were caught up with finding me a new name,
said you renamed all your loved ones.
I heard, *He loves me* and blushed at the thought
of being christened again so late in life.
We were walking up my stairs to disrobe
for the first time when midflight you held me,
My Tanara, and stopped my breath with your tongue.
In the weeks to come as I danced flatfooted in your dense air
and you bought me new perfume, said my old one smelled
like mosquito repellent, refined my diet to suit your taste
for raw delights, suggested I cut the colour out my hair –
it made me look wild and not like myself,
ironies of all ironies: I, who taught that book about
men locking women in confined spaces, didn't realize
I had climbed into its pages.

LET THIS BE YOUR PRAISE

THE MERCHANT OF FEATHERS I

got the short end of the stick,
found ill-repute in the under-appreciation
of his work. No one praises
the feathers stuffed into pillows,
the wispy base of dreams,
the floating density of mattresses
that cushion day's exertion.
No wonder he stuffed his stock
with rocks.
But the merchant of feathers is now a woman
selling softness in these hard times,
stretching rations to feed the multitudes.
She is the domestic worker
tireless in her cleaning of the country's sores.
She is the woman whose song
lifts like mist from the Blue Mountains.
Sometimes she chants and hits her head
against walls, but never mind,
she is standing between us and evil spirits,
her body a buffer in the night's dead breeze.
So often, we praise her for being the rock
but let us praise her, too, for bringing feathers
to buoy us up, beauty so easy now to forget.

ON THE OTHER SIDE OF MADNESS

To the man of unsound mind who lives in the bushes
below my window, I hear you each night howling
against the still breath of rustling leaves
and brittle twigs that break underfoot.

I push off sleep to sit up with you, sending
wishes of calm through these concrete walls.
I know how the voices inhabit,
the pure dread of seeing red everywhere:
in the moon's eyes, in the belly of stars.

As you chant your lullaby of bad words,
I leaf through the Bible searching for psalms
to whisper across the divide.
I want to throw you a lighter
on nights when you misplace yours.

I know how a lighter can ignite bush fire
to ward off mosquitoes and evil spirits;
holy lighter needed to cook on the nights
you remember hunger.

But I am afraid to throw salvation at your feet,
in case you seek me out come morning,
throw stones as sign of thanks,

or the lighter landing at your feet
will force you to look up, thinking God
lives in a brand new town-house complex.
At last He has found you.
Halleluiah, wrap up your small bundle and climb.

DINING AT CUSTOMS

Miss Gloria had risen early that morning,
cooked the goat she had killed and seasoned
the night before in a Dutch pot over a coal fire
in her cousin Doris's back yard right between
the coconut trees that lived through three hurricanes.

She would eat it when she got in from the airport,
the yellow spicy meat, fragments of sunlight
settling in her stomach, warming her bones with
memories of somewhere other than this place
where William, her son, recipient of scholarship
to Harvard had settled, then sent for her.
She arrived during summer, pleased that here, too,
there was heat. The first winter she spoke to no one,
betrayed by the suddenness of cold, the imperialism
of snow, the son who learned to live with below zero.

For five years she cleaned, cared for his zombie children,
took orders from his wife, who Miss Gloria swears
is secretly a man. One day, head tied, brown socks
pulled up to her knees, arms akimbo, she said,
"William, I going home for a little holiday.
Too much people dying behind my back."

For two months, she sat on a verandah
regaling the district with Uncle Sam stories:
how everywhere have elevator, bright lights,
fast service, how her grandchildren smart
and her daughter-in-law pretty like money
and soft-spoken like any English lady.

And now this customs man, face pale like alabaster,
telling her she can't carry unfrozen curried goat through customs.
Miss Gloria takes off her maroon sweater, spreads it

on the industrial carpet, laps her long floral skirt between
her thighs, eases her body to the floor. She sorry
she don't have fork or glass full of lemonade,
sorry Doris not here so they can chat and eat, sorry
this man don't come from anywhere, sorry he going try
to stop her as she put the first piece of meat to her mouth.
And she thinking is that she waiting for long, long time.

AT THE NURSING HOME

"It's your favourite!" And he smiles. "Is Tanya,
must be Tanya." He pulls my name
out of some small working portion of his brain,
conjures me up out of dying cells.
I know I am the straw he clutches at,
the fixed in the midst of fading signifiers,
the one he remembers against his body's
own efforts at forgetting.
I know he may not see the past
with my clear lenses:
meals he cooked me, jokes he shared
in baritone voice still bellowing in my bones,
lessons he taught me – like a man
is supposed to protect a woman,
so if a mad man jumps in the open back of a truck
carrying six granddaughters, the man who is driving
can stop without warning and pull him out
with the force of gods and demons.
He may not remember
he taught me my first words,
"Plup up" as I echoed his "Shut up",
or that he taught me how to drink rum
with the fanfare of cowboys in Westerns.
His love for me does not depend on the details,
and when he dies
I know that despite all his sins committed
against his children,
he will find some favour
because he taught one girl that love
is larger than the space we live in.

TO THE MAN WHO TENDS
MY GRANDMOTHER'S GRAVE

I give you thanks for knowing the ways of the living,
how it is important for my mother to know her mother
has not been forgotten: last week a son brought three
faux flowers, wept like a child over her grave; the week
before Mrs. B, on her way to visit her daughter cut down
by sugar, stopped for a brief chat, laughing like old times.
I give you thanks for the plot of grass, perpetually green
in a place famous for water lock-offs and parched earth.
I give you thanks for stooping to Brillo-polish her silver
tombstone so we see ourselves in the sheen.
I give you thanks for carrying the red dirt from all these
graves into your house each night, showing your children
that we are all half spirit, composites of the living and the dead.
I give you thanks for taking the crumpled bills, small
payment for backbreaking work in the sun, with a smile;
even when this exchange is infrequent, like the rain here.
I give you thanks for knowing the slight bend of a body
carrying grief, the quiet before flood. Last Sunday we came
with my father to visit his brother freshly laid in the earth,
another grave for you to tend; we thought he was handling
it well, he could drive us home. Quickly you ushered me over,
"Him can't drive. Him soon bruk down bad, bad." My mother
drove, my father became the water within him.
And you who tend these graves, may your death find you
among familiar faces, grateful recipients of your tending.

MELBA SPEAKS (AGAIN)

When the rum back died
his outside children descended
like the plague
turned the house upside down
looking for money
under the divan
inside biscuit tins
old clothes
even the Bible.
I don't stop them.
Life teach me
you can live half your life
with a man
and don't know
his secrets.

TO THE MAN WHO STILL TENDS
MY GRANDMOTHER'S GRAVE

When you were shot,
the green grass around grandma's tomb
went bristle and brown.
Spirits gathered to pray for your safe return,
sent emissaries to search you down
and bind you back together again.
We call you "Kid", not knowing
if it's your right name.
Some men have names for work,
for strangers who hand them crumpled bills,
and names for home, for the ones who really see them
when they are wounded and alive.
When we visit this expanding cemetery,
you are never close, always someone has to fetch you.
You appear from behind the old church or one big tree
or dug-out hillside being flattened for new dead.
Guardian of graves, shot in the leg by a common thief,
halfway out your house with DVD player,
perhaps pissed there was so little for him to steal.
They will not pull you into the earth, into the four corners
of cedar and nails so easily.

LET THIS BE YOUR PRAISE

And what is praise but the offering up of one's self,
the daily rituals: waking to the stream of light seeping in
under the bedroom door, dressing slowly, humming Marley's
"Three Little Birds" or a made-up melody,
cursing the traffic and the heat – the unbearable brazenness
of the morning sun – punctuating your profanities
with pleas for forgiveness. When you were a child,
your mother threatened to wash your mouth with soap.
You have not forgotten how a mouth can sully everything,
its desire to be perfect and how often it fails.
At work you smile with the girl who asks stupid questions,
you imagine she has unpaid bills, a wayward child;
you imagine you are more alike than different.
You cut your nails at your desk, laugh when someone falls,
eat lunch too quickly, take Tums for the indigestion.
In the evening you drink peppermint tea, watch TV and
when your eyes grow heavy you say a quick word
of prayer, a thank you for another full day, a request that you
not be killed in your sleep. Maybe, you squeeze in an orgasm.
And if this is not praise, this simple act of living, if this is not
enough, then let us lie here and do nothing and see
what God has to say about that.

SUNDAY DRIVE OUT
For AJ

We enter the mountains at Papine
just as we did on our first date
when you took me hiking up Newcastle
and a storm caught us on the path.
Today, we have no clear destination
in mind. We wind down the windows,
peer at the city below, slow
down to give the lazing goats
a chance to move out the way.
We turn on to side roads
etched between sky and precipice,
find a revivalist church where
the road meets shrubbery and
the turbaned women spill out
like white orchids on a painter's easel.
We reverse in the middle of their stares,
careful not to drive over the feet of women
who worship this close to God.
We find another off-beaten road;
it ends in a house with a sign that reads,
"Do not trespass. You've been warned."
I wonder aloud who builds his house
in the middle of nowhere on a road
dug out and eroding, who lives this far up.
Is this how you make love survive:
carve a concrete edifice close to the sky?
I make you promise we will never live
in a place like this, even though the air
up here is cool to the breath.
I want us to face what awaits us
down below. I want to leave this mountain
as a verdant backdrop, an occasional respite.

GRACE

On days when I worship you
more than I should,
when your mouth is my only altar,
and time
is measured by how long
you spend between me,
or the width of your absence;

on days when I cannot distinguish our bodies
and even mirrors deceive me,
when I remember God
only on the cusp of coming,
when His name is your name
and the afterlife is a place
we create;

on days when all sounds lead me
to your voice,
the night jasmine carries your smell,
when everything is your skin
and I tongue books
and trees and strangers;

on days when longing is a form of madness
and the sun inside me swells,
when faith is knowing you'll return
for more of this
and naked we are our water selves;

on days when I worship you more
than I should, I am glad
God is merciful, benevolent,
full of grace.

JUST KISSING

dislodged by your tongue
paper-thin grape skin
on my tongue
lone remnant
from the tart bunch I ate
that morning
perhaps it had been hiding
behind tonsils or molars
I held it up to the light
flicked it on to the carpet
gave you my tongue again
we kissed and kissed
and I wondered what else
that tongue of yours would find

LOVE DONE DID IT

Love intoxicated my tongue

        painted the birds' songs B'dazzled Blue

    Love made our bed

           sent butterflies for your halo

Love slayed the dragons
           in my dreams

    kissed the frog

Love lifted me

    off Kingston's concrete

           sent me flying

    over the Blue Lagoon

           Love burned the past down to dust

    proclaimed itself the gospel

        Love made a bullet

of my heart

        Love dug trenches

           was unafraid of the word *fallow*

Love came

                          purple-caped and panting

          on the wings of a mother's prayer

NIGHT NURSE

As the crowd dissipates
and the hour hand lurches to 3 am
and we are tired
of dodging our intentions,
I come to you,
pulled like lightning to zinc.
We forget ourselves –
children, blemishes, spouses,
bosses, leaky faucets –
press against each other,
my back against your chest,
your chin nuzzled in my hair,
your hand trailing deferred dreams
along the front of my thighs.
I singe my backside
into the swell of your groin.
We are not moving to the rhythm.
We do not care for the deejay's gimmicks.
We are sound system enough –
each circle of our waists, a low-lying bass,
an insistent pounding,
a lick and a drizzle of strings.
We know we must leave here together,
crisscross our steps as if
going in separate directions
but not yet, not before you spin me around
so in this moment I can see
how much you wish
love found us with different lives.

SAID BY A DJ AT A DOWNTOWN DANCE

Big up yuhself if yuh pum pum tight like mosquito coffin!

I want mine lined with purple velvet. I want the men I have killed
to rise again, to sing halleluiahs in praise of this sweet spot,
smaller than a melon seed, a discarded tooth, a dew drop.
Smaller than an eyeball's socket, a screw, the space between seconds.
Smaller than a candle wick, an atom, a fly. Perhaps a needle's eye?
Tight like starched linen, a market bus, a single mother's budget.
Tight like a tightrope walker's rope, a strangler's hand on the throat.
Tight like a child's grip on a candy stick, an inner city gang.
I read that long ago women in parts of Africa lined their pum pums
with toothpaste. Their men loved the friction, the fire small sacrifice
for a return customer, happy breadwinner, bloated ego.
The other day I heard a man dis a woman: "Gwey, u pum pum long like…"
We are measured by the length and width,
the colour and texture, the dryness and the wetness.
Oh, how we pray as women for resilience, to bounce back
in the face of dicks and pricks and big-headed babies.
And in the dance, surrounded by men, we flash up our lighters,
point our fingers in gun salute, shout "RAAEEE" in case
we are mistaken for women whose pum pums could hold
the coffin, the congregation, the choir, the hearse.

KILL HIM WID IT, EH EH

Jack Ass say di world nuh level

There are men paying fat women to squash them

You see mi dying trial

Every hoe have him stick a bush

The bigger the woman, the sweeter the pleasure

The woman don't have to give up no front

Just lie down on the man until him heart come close to stopping

I guess is like strangling

Whatever tickle your fancy

But all praise to the fat woman who can squash a man good

Because one wrong move and you literally kill a man wid it

When him deep breathing, you have to know the difference

Between orgasm and dying, you have to know the true weight of a pound of flesh

How much a heart can take, how to ease yourself down part by part

Is not easy to divide yourself so

Is not easy to walk with so much power in your flesh

THE MERCHANT OF FEATHERS III

He shall cover thee with his feathers, and under his wings shalt thou trust:
His truth shall be thy shield and buckler. Psalm 91, v 4

Street Vibes Night at The Building and men are hungry
for amnesia floating on the wings of weed smoke
in the soft words whispered by her hips.
Here is where she holds court
in a sky-blue bikini, knee-high silver boots.
She smiles at the DJ, sequins spill from her mouth.
He selects new tunes to match the rhythm of her stance.
She is bad gyal and mermaid, windmill and still breeze.
The men line up to sip the dreams she sells.
Red Bull cans like guns in their hands,
dark glasses shield the torches in their eyes.
Her peacock lashes flutter proud against the canvas
of her store-bought skin. The first man crosses
the divide, holds her from behind.
She bends forward, her head a cornrowed pedestal
for the cascading curls of a jet black wig.
She will save the dutty wine for the last in line.
This one gets the slow anointing of tick tocking
hips, the panorama of an arched back.
One by one they bury the week's worries
in the tight space between their bodies.
Drenched in rum-soaked sweat, they glide
over the thumping melodies, the loaded words.
When night turns to morning, she sends them home,
feathers falling behind them.

they will not say I "passed" or "transitioned".
Like your Mavis, I want to be *dead*.
    I want that word to sound in the bones
of my enemies.
    I want a weeping and a wailing and a gnashing of teeth,
the clouds to pour down mourning.
    I want grown men to fall into
the laps of strangers: proof I was their great love.
    I want to lie in state with a line of viewers
wrapped around Kingston's corners.
    I want a parade
with jugglers and hookers and poets;
no humble burial
with me burned into the edges of a small box
and a procession of Anglo-Saxon imitators
singing classic choruses. No.
    I want drums and dragons
breathing fire from a pulpit draped in purple.
When I die,
let outsiders not be mistaken.
Here is a body that is no more and
    I want you to grieve for my flesh
that knew what it was to be pinched
and squeezed, bitten, adored.
Those who know how I lived,
sometimes dangling from high wires
but always out in the open,
let them stand and say "Amen!"
appoint a professional to roll up and down
the red-carpeted centre aisle,
her humongous breasts spilling wine.
    I want trumpets and saxophones,
a congregation of stilettoes and lace.
    I want tears to turn the pews into the night sea

and when they close the coffin
and the dapper pallbearers take their place,
    I want ten thousand doves released
and a horde of women clad in Pentecostal white
to bear down on me like a flock of sheep
as if telling the earth, they will not let me go down
without a fight.

NOTES

p. 12
Kukumkum: Jamaican Dialect word meaning "extremely skinny".

p. 27
Matie: Jamaican term for "the woman on the side" or "the mistress".

p. 46.
Scandal bags: Jamaican name for plastic bags.

p. 47.
Every Hoe Have Him Stick a Bush: Jamaican proverb meaning that there is a suitable partner for everyone; even the most unlikely persons can find someone to love them.

ABOUT THE AUTHOR

In Kei Miller's anthology, *New Caribbean Poetry* (2007), Tanya Shirley was selected as one of eight poets in whose hands the future of Caribbean poetry was secure. Her debut collection, *She Who Sleeps With Bones* (Peepal Tree Press, 2009) not only garnered many very positive reviews but was named by the *Jamaica Gleaner* as one of the year's best sellers. Her work is published in several anthologies and she has read her poems in Venezuela, Canada, the U.S.A., England, Scotland and the Caribbean.

She was awarded an MFA in Creative Writing from the University of Maryland, USA. She currently teaches in the Department of Literatures in English, UWI, Mona where she is also a PhD candidate. Tanya Shirley is also proud to be a Cave Canem Fellow.

ALSO BY TANYA SHIRLEY

She Who Sleeps with Bones
ISBN: 9781845230876; pp. 76; pub. 2009; price: £7.99

In Tanya Shirley's S*he Who Sleeps With Bones*, the hauntings of memory
and the spiritual lead us to eloquently shaped epiphanies that turn
what appear at on the surface to be simple and tidy stories into
profound meditations on the human condition. Shirley acts as a
witness to the lives of those around her, yet she is a biased witness,
one who has become so enmeshed in the lives of her "characters"
that gradually we become convinced that she has erased the lines that
would allow us to distinguish her from the people who enter her
work. The collection is anchored by a series of spiritual poems that
beautifully enact the mysteries of inner sight and clairvoyance of a
poet who is a reluctant seer, who comes from a family of seers.

Her reluctance arises from the toll that sight brings to the poet –
the burden of feeling, and speaking the truths that haunt. And yet for
all its spiritual intelligence, these are poems of earthy sensuality and
celebratory humor that are fully rooted in the every day details of
living, loving, fearing, laughing and hoping.

Shirley's poems are beautifully crafted and they reveal her deft
handling of syntax and musicality. She is as meticulous in her choice
of words and images as she is in her honesty of emotion and risk-
taking.

Ultimately, however, it is the resilience of her joy that remains
with us after each poem – for all its complications, (and there are
many explored here – deaths of dear friends and relatives, the
anxieties of being an alien in another country, the perils of unre-
quited love, the importance of size in sexual play, and the premoni-
tions of tragedy) the world is ultimately full of wonder and joy for
Tanya Shirley, a joy that she manages to make sublimely contagious.